BRASS BAND TO FOLLOW

BRASS BAND
TO FOLLOW

POEMS

BRYAN WALPERT

OTAGO UNIVERSITY PRESS
Te Whare Tā o Te Wānanga o Ōtākou

For Nancy

Published by Otago University Press
Te Whare Tā o Te Wānanga o Ōtākou
533 Castle Street
Dunedin, New Zealand
university.press@otago.ac.nz
www.otago.ac.nz/press

First published 2021
Copyright © Bryan Walpert
The moral rights of the author have been asserted.

ISBN 978-1-99-004804-3

Editor: Lynley Edmeades
Cover photograph: Shutterstock

Printed in New Zealand by Southern Colour Print, Dunedin

In Freudian terms, Zweig sees in Dostoyevsky an honesty about the longing for plenitude that haunts all of us throughout life in various ways and which becomes especially pressing in middle age, for then one most acutely realizes the absolute hopelessness of the thought that it will ever be satisfied.

—Christopher Hamilton, *Middle Age*

When questioned they tell us youth lasts to 50 years, and middle age is around 80 years, and people enjoy plenitude and abundance for the remainder of life.

—Gayle Redfern, *Ancient Wisdoms: Exploring the Mysteries and Connections*

CONTENTS

BRASS BAND TO FOLLOW

PROMPTED

Begin with

something simple, something near,
not too near, it has to be distant
or you have to be distant enough from it
to see it coolly, like the moon.
No, stay away from the moon.
Okay, I don't know, a vegetable
in the garden on one of these final nights
of summer, so cool on a night like this.
Yes, good, though a bit less distant,
come in so we can see it: the lettuce, say,
yes, that's the idea but, no, a bit on the surface.
Okay, how about the kohlrabi. Well, a bit exotic,
self-conscious, too much about how much
you know. For god's sake the carrot then.
Yes, good, now what about the carrot,
which you are keeping at just the right distance
on one of the last nights of summer,
the buzz of your daughter's electric toothbrush
slipping through the open bathroom window
past the small bugs attracted to the light
that will smatter the ceiling like the inverse of stars,
light slipping into the back yard, onto the vegetable garden—
she's brushing the last of the lettuce from her teeth,
half of them baby teeth still, maybe fewer.
Now don't get too close: your wife has probably combed
your daughter's hair by now, read your son a story,
the light off in his room, the light gone largely, too,
from the sky, the shapes starting from this distance
to lose their distinctions. It's easier now to see the moon
you are meant to avoid, afraid you might have missed
saying goodnight. No, think about the vegetables,
the kohlrabi, for instance, its strange history,

stick with the kohlrabi, which sits there dumbly,
a kind of model of forbearance. Is this about
forbearance. No, don't rush to judgement, just look,
though it's dark now, a shred of moon
cast against the unforgiving dark,
their mother having by now locked the door,
while you sit here contemplating
what is hidden, untended, known
but not really, moving away bit by bit
like the moon. What you would give
for the buzz of a toothbrush, a call in the night,
but there is inside and outside, a decision
you made long ago. Look, you've got
the sky and the stars, the vegetable
nature of time, which you really don't have
a handle on at all, so just focus on the last
cool night of summer, all that is unknown
deep in their beds, though be sure to focus
on the coolness, stay outside, not too close,
keep a reasonable distance, a few feet of darkness,
the thickness of a wall, don't move
an inch, you'll get there.

Prompted

There are twelve words I'm meant to use
in this poem. Try to guess what they are.
I'll start you off with one: *poplar*. Another is *twigs*.
I'm no Keats, but obviously this is an autumnal poem,
the branches bare. Forlorn is the third word.
Tricky—adjectives always are—though
not as tricky as slipping in the word escarpment.
Too Latinate, for one. Also, I had to look it up.
I've already forgotten about autumn. I'm thinking
about your easy laughter, the crease it carved
in your otherwise unworried forehead,
the church next door ringing ten o'clock Mass
while we scarfed our French toast, the poplar
in full flower. Scarf is not one of the words,
by the way, though distant is. So is leaves.
I'm determined to be original. Can I use
the word 'left' instead? Actually,
there was plenty of autumn to go around.
Amnesia, another word I'm meant to use
(along with laughter and crease)
is as often self-inflicted. An escarpment
is formed when the earth's crust fractures.
This might be an opportunity to use
my third-to-last word, rock. But, first,
think about the metaphoric reverberation
of a word like escarpment. This is not just
a way to use the penultimate word reverberate.
I mean, really think about its reverberation
in our lives, yours and mine. If it helps,
replace 'earth' with 'world'
then remove the too-particular 'crust'.
There you are. Finally, the word tongue.

There are many obvious ways to insert
tongue into a poem about you.
This isn't that sort of poem.
This is the sort of poem where we imagine
how you'd read this if you still lived with me
in the house by the church with the poplar
shedding its leaves in sudden small eruptions,
like laughter. How your very tone,
like the angle of light those Sunday mornings,
would suggest the shift in season,
how your tongue would roll around these words
like the orbit of a distant rock. Ten o'clock again.
Screw Keats. *Forlorn, forlorn, forlorn.*

Tangent

Triangle

Afternoon and its folding
of light
into evening.

Rectangle

The weekend,
deserted island with its cut edges,
the shadow of a box
she'd held waist high.

Angle

An arm sweeps
a newly emptied room at first light
in shifting degrees of elbow
as if, by division,
we might embrace depths like a wing
or bend like water.

Relativities

I am standing in front of a gas range
is a sentence Einstein once wrote
to make a point about time and change
(though check out the lone footnote
at the bottom of that page).
I wish I were growing clever.
Instead, I continue to age.
Now, it seems, has a fairly short tether.
There was a girl, of course. She left on a train
as I watched from the grassy embankment.
What Einstein meant is hard to explain,
though I position his book around the apartment.
I'm very like Einstein, without the hair.
That is, I'm waiting for the kettle.
Time takes its time from here to there.
Look, Einstein was once just this fellow
in a patent office, doodling the map
of one idea: there are few absolutes.
(Though don't tell a girl she's gone fat.
The universe holds certain truths.)
This is not going well at all.
The speed of light, where you put the phone,
the lyrics of a song you can nearly recall:
there are things you know you've known.
The long-dead stars, the setting sun.
She wore orange blossom. Or was it rose?
Small wonder she's gone—
you know how that goes.
Look, you haven't read the footnote
and probably never will
(but check me on the opening quote).
Her note to me is sealed up still.

Some things you know you know.
Einstein contemplating a pot.
The empty chair, time's wingèd flow.
The water is nearly hot.

Two Mornings

I.

the cat yawns

yellow light
over the back deck

swallows
the sounds
of birds

stirring
like stars
from shadows

yesterday's scent
hangs
above a puddle
of merlot

an idea
about clouds

II.
since you

light's edges
till the air

your shadow

flowers
an exhale

gathers rain
the sunrise

petals on the floor

Orb to be Named Later

Don't look up. I'm trying to avoid symbol
here, trying to avoid even its hint, the nuance,
the million meanings winking like—don't say it,
it's almost, you know, in the same area,
it rises into my lines like—what the hell, I need
a new vocabulary. Guttural? Gluttonous? Selenite?
I'm trying to say something to you.
Who am I to dare? To wax?
See, it's irresistible. I'm the tide,
the lover, the Renaissance hack wading
through centuries of bedclothes just
to be here, to tell you in one-syllable gutturals
what you know, what you look like.
But I won't, I won't. It's just that it's so there,
gluttonous for digression, a rotunda of glaze.
And I'm here, which is to say at that border
where they stamp yearn on your passport
and wink you through. Put it in drive,
slam the pedal with a steel-tip, still
it bounces in the rear-view. Still,
it hovers like a bad idea,
like what you once said you thought
I was going to say and nearly did,
the night at our backs, you'll never
know how close we came, how close
you seemed, though now look at you,
you're, like, 238,855 miles away.

In the lull

now, after the heavy rain—the kind
whose sudden arrival, whose shocking
weight, even if forecast, sends anything
alive scurrying for cover without care
for dignity—when it is still
possible to hear the water sluice
along drainpipes, through gutters,
along any slanted surface, he watches it
puddle in the grass he would cut as she
watched him through that same window
from the house on a hill whose lawns
rise now unimpeded like any perverted
vision of freedom: hers, an absence
she made clear always clouded
the horizon, weather whose arrival,
more so for being forestalled,
haunted every blooming
pōhutukawa, each bloody magnolia,
only these words a final
awkward rushing after,
water whispering a memory
of what it once was even as it ebbs
by following in reverse the road
they'd climb to get home each day,
their mouths dry from the effort
of its long, implacable gradient.

Two Flowers

Heartleaf Arnica
(*Arnica cordifolia*)

Pressed
to your thigh,
will cleanse
blood.

Taken inside,
will rise
like mercury.

You have
a decision to make

so I fill
the silence
with information.

Consider this flower:
know what it is

to have two hearts
opposed

at the base
of one body.

Monkshood
(*Aconitum columbianum*)

Even alone
elevated

there are only
so many
ways to hide

desire.

This one too has something
to teach:

don't place trust
too fully in peace,
its poison
a slow sedative.

So few words
between us today.

See it nodding
in the wind
as if to
a question
we've not voiced,
or in meditation
on the answer.

Transporting

In my old apartment,
the ghosts of my former
furniture evade dust,
the short mahogany
bureau cured of its gout,
the La-Z-Boy of its
broken foot. My footprints
on the hardwood floors dance
as a younger man can.
I read today that some
scientists transported
a beam of light from one
side of a slim bench to
another in their lab,
not like a flashlight, but
replicated it, whole.
It works because a par-
ticle split becomes two
selves that even apart
feel the same touch, as twins
separated at birth
will grow the same dark beards,
marry the same women
(Diane instead of Dawn),
light the same cigarettes,
listen to Hank Williams.
We, too, might be remade
across this room now that
we're two: the one we are
and the one we'll recall,
though it's hard to say who
is the original

and who is the copy.
The experiment has
not gone this far, but it's
just a matter of time.
Even now, miles from here,
my old television
replays the past; my lamp,
with its once-fraying cord,
recalls itself so well
it could burst into song.

Gross Anatomy

The dead flesh awaiting touch,
the sun rarely seen,
spending itself at a speed
we can only approach.

Mornings he arrives early,
sits among them
in the warming months,
these numb minutes, the tick

of the faucet. Beneath each sheet
he imagines a twin he has
never known. The clock
of the self, having

slowed to seconds,
seems to spin
ever more slowly,
the others arriving now,

sensations breaking into silence
that stirs, like wind on water,
spring surfacing as so many
souls burst into bodies.

Tranquil

I'll probably cut this line,
maybe this one, too, and the next,
the one that describes the blanket—
it's no good, you keep it,
the line, I mean, though you can have
the old blanket, too, whose rough wool
scratched us all winter on that couch
you've taken with the music and the terrier,
leaving only a few unmatched dishes
and a memory I no longer want:
the day the snow surprised the city—
you at one end of the park,
me at the other, dog by your side,
the spot we were to meet in the middle
an objective correlative of all compromises
with which we would surely collude,
the whole silly city out shovelling,
the white world masquerading
as some sort of moment—take it all, crate it
up with the photos, pop it all in the boot
along with all that we once felt
for one another, take everything
but this poem you'll never see
me cut line by line:
fold, spindle, mutilate—it's going,
you're in charge, my queen, my subject
no longer, once I've cut these last few
about the books we'd planned to read, the dog
I'll tell you now I hated, the day I can't stop
thinking about, which ended with a blanket,
an old couch, and started with the snow
laid out between us like this cold, blank page.

ONLY THINE EYES

Evolution

When you can bear me no longer,
you seek refuge, like the poets, in nature,
your favourite plant here the ponga,
a giant fern that is not exactly a tree

but not exactly not one, either,
an oddity that comes from living
on an island, cut off and forced
to make do. What to do

but develop strange habits, seek
beauty in what it is to survive
the sea and the gales, to find grudging
admiration for those trees

that poison one another, steal sap,
or, like the rātā, smother a neighbour.
Fully half of New Zealand's trees
require male and female to reproduce,

more than in any other country.
You need each other in a place
like this, but, yes, close quarters,
easy to get on one another's

nerves, cut off from the world,
unless you develop thicker skin,
as have the karaka and ngaio,
their leaves leathery enough

to survive the daily insults
of the winds, their surfaces waxy
to prevent, when injury occurs,
the salt settling in.

Micrographia

or some Physiological Descriptions of minute bodies made by
magnifying glasses with Observations and Inquiries thereupon.

after Robert Hooke

An attempt for the explication of this experiment

We might begin with what we
call *Congruity*. No, bear with me.
The *highest property* of *Congruity*
is a cohesion of the parts,
a kind of *attraction* and *tenacity*,
there surely being as many ways
of making *Harmonies* and *Discords*
with these, as there may be
with *musical strings*, say of this quartet—
a fugue, Bach perhaps?—
playing on the concert station
you have yet again chosen
from the passenger seat to replace
the more robust contemporary music
on the station I had initially selected.
What I am suggesting, thus,
is that some bodies are *united*
more *firmly*, others *loosened*
from each other by every *vibrative* motion.
It is perhaps also fair
to say the driver tends to make these
sorts of decisions, not of course by law
but, rather, by convention. In sum,
those that are *similar*, will, like so many
equal musical strings equally stretched,
vibrate together in a kind of *Harmony* or *Unison*,

whereas others that are *dissimilar*,
like so many *strings out of tune*,
so *untuned*, as it were,
to each other, that they *cross* and *jar*,
consequently, *cannot agree* together,
will *fly back* from each other. We see
therefore—let me finish—the reason
for the sympathy or uniting of some bodies,
and for the antipathy or flight of others
from each other: for *Congruity*
seems nothing but a *Sympathy*,
Incongruity an *Antipathy* of bodies.
Hence similar bodies once united
will not easily part, and dissimilar bodies
once disjoined will not easily unite again.
No, this is not just about getting one's way.
Please at least turn it down.

Of incongruity

That is, the property
of a body, by which
it will not be united with any other.
Maybe this is confusing.
We don't, by way of example,
have to look any further than the rain
parting the air beyond the kitchen window,
or the bubbles of air conveyed
beneath the meniscus of the water
accumulated in the guttering
I know I am overdue in clearing out.
Or consider the few drops of common salad oil,
applied in the meal concluded moments ago,
now separating to the surface
of the dish submerged in the sink
I stand before as,
the washing not yet done,
I shut off the taps to better
hear what you might have said
from the other room
to which it seems of late
you find yourself drifting.

Of the bookworm

Among the greater animals
there is a lesser body much conversant
among books and papers
which, upon their removal in the summer,
is often observed nimbly to scud
and pack away to some lurking cranny,
the better to protect itself
from any appearing dangers, real or imagined.
Its head appears big, blunt,
its body a taper, smaller and smaller,
being shaped in time almost like a carrot
rooted always in the dark,
or, in seated position, a question.
How it feeds upon the paper and the books,
finding, perhaps, a convenient nourishment,
able yet further to work upon those stubborn
difficult parts, and reduce them into another form.
And indeed, when I consider what a heap of dust
this little creature (which is one of the teeth of Time)
conveys into its entrails, I cannot choose
but admire the excellent contrivance of nature,
in placing in some of us as this such a fire,
as is continually nourished and supplied
and fomented by the bellows of the lungs.
And in so contriving that the very spending and wasting
be instrumental to the procuring and collecting
of more materials to augment and cherish itself,
does this not seem, my love, to be
the principal end of all the contrivances observable
in that world you so often insist, as
you do today—*the sun*, you say, *the yard*—

that I *for one goddamn minute* recognise
exists beyond the page?

Of a small needle

which, however easily
it makes its way through
the softness of a body,
is less sharp than it seems.
It reveals itself on close
inspection to be broad
and blunt as any careless remark
that, if examined more acutely,
is marked by the rudeness
and bungling of art,
the question being,
not to put too fine a point
upon it, love, whether one wants
primarily to pain or to pierce.

Of the pores of bodies

Even a stone,
to the naked

eye a closed object,

is perforated,
interstitial,
might with some contrivance

be discovered to be open.

Once I took a large Kettering stone and—

well, I can see you are growing
distracted, that perhaps you
have other things on your mind,

judging by the nightgown—
new, isn't it?—
your awkward position on the bed.

Anyway, it is a small matter
beside the several

arguments I could bring
to show that even solid bodies
are not solid

and evince
how light is conveyed—
are you listening?—
from the lucid
to the unenlightened.

Of the razor

that each morning we take
so casually to our throats,
it would seem hard to say much
without perhaps giving
too much weight to too little.
Still, worlds in grains of sand, etc.,
peering closer, we will find
that polished on a grinding stone,
its edge appears a plowed field,
with its many parallels, ridges and furrows.
Step back or up a scale
and the razor, too, must be seen as a plow,
grooming the fields of the face.
Such cutting back reminds us that
we, like the edge of a razor,
consist of an infinity of small broken surfaces.
How strange each morning to place one to the neck,
to bring such roughness to bear—
removal a kind of dutiful forgetting,
as I dutifully attempt this morning
not to recall the manner in which
your voice carried the previous evening
through this same door, indistinct,
my having kicked it closed,
as you enumerated the various ways
a man can get something rather simple
rather wrong, a point I might
wish to debate more deeply but
perhaps will not.
Strange, for if such an edge existed writ large
as it appeared through the lens
it could scarcely serve to cleave wood
much less shave unless, of course—

as one might reflect to one's self
in the mirror, considering
whether to raise the point
to her again, to offer
an alternative point of view—
it were used the way it is said Charon
once employed an axe
to chop the beard from the chin
of a philosopher whose unnecessary gravity
he feared would overturn his ferry,
casting its cargo into depths
even he thought best not to plumb.

Of the full stop

Even this,
so perfectly shaped
to the eye,
is not the end

of perception.
Look closer.
The most smoothly engraved,
of copperplate or type,
appears, when you peer
close enough, to be so many
furrows and holes
through which one might
thread with a needle
of thought a thousand objections,
the way the thousand threads
that compose a shirt—

draped so elegantly
on the body of someone
very like you
reading a sentiment
that should have been delivered
so long ago
and must now be
conveyed by such distance—

appear at first blush
an unbroken broad cloth
but might yet be unwoven,

while one scrawled by pencil
is revealed through that lens
to be as unformed
as any story
whose expression
it might yet not be
too late not to draw
to a close.

Migration

Travelling in flocks is an old adaptation.
Stick, if you can, close behind one another.
Flying this far is not so bad in formation.

Consider the crowds at Wellington station:
the small girl in tears, the harried mother.
Travelling in flocks is an old adaptation.

Though in truth this is about our situation.
The details—not worth the bother.
Flying this far is not so bad in formation.

How'd we get here? I mean expectations.
House, kids, the lawns in good weather.
Travelling in flocks is an old adaptation.

Your blame or mine, this grand immigration?
Easy to get one's self in a lather
flying this far on bad information.

I suppose we all need a last iteration.
You get where you get when you take on a lover.
Travelling in flocks is an old adaptation.
Flying this far is not so bad in formation.

The fantail

is a famously sociable bird, happy
to come within a metre or so
though difficult to capture
even with a camera as my wife
tries now—click, *damn,* click, *wait—*
the two kids and I standing on the grass
in the front garden in our best clothes,
waiting for her to place the camera on the rail
of the deck and set the timer so we can
take the annual Easter family photo.
The tradition also encompasses
my distracting the kids so my wife
can place the foil-wrapped chocolate eggs
for them to find glinting in the grass,
in the crook of small trees, on the bench
of the deck. Eight and five, we don't have
much time left for them to think this
evidence of the generosity of a large
bunny—the eldest has already at times
expressed her doubts, duly suppressed
now for the sake of the sweets.
For how long? It will take, as it turns out,
several attempts to get the family photo.
In one, my daughter's eyes are closed.
In another, my wife has just barely made it
into the frame when the camera's
automatic shutter moves. You can tell
in the photo that it's a beautiful morning
moving into noon and by the length
of the lawn that it's a sweet spot
of sunshine after days of rain.
My wife caught running into

the photograph, half-in, half-out.
The kids getting impatient.
The fantail flitting from one branch to the next,
threatening always to fly across the year of the yard.
Hold on one minute, she says, moving
the camera lens here, then there.
Hold on, she says, I've got you.

Experiments Touching Cold

or, An experimental history of cold whereunto is annexed
An Account of Freezing

after Robert Boyle

As to those that are kill'd with Cold, our Author informs us, that they
perish'd by two differing kinds of death. For some being not sufficiently
fortifi'd against the cold by their own internal heat, nor competently
arm'd against it by Furs, Injunctions, and other external means ... But
the other way whereby cold destroys men, is that, which is the most
remarkable in our Author, and though less sudden is more cruel.
  —Robert Boyle, 'Of the strange Effects of Cold'

Experiments touching cold (1)

If you needed any evidence
that even so extremely close
a medium as glass,
as Boyle eloquently put it,
is not able to hinder
the transmission of cold,
it is here centuries later
in this second-storey window
through which you look
today onto the garden
where even in such intemperate
conditions she works her shears
and pulls up weeds,
less—it would seem by the evidence
of such weather as there is today—
to ensure the efficacy of the task
than to gather to herself
the necessary space unavailable
because not wholly physical

in a house otherwise occupied.
Though it is tempting
to rap upon the window, its attempt
would simply leave her in the difficult
position of deciding whether
to acknowledge the fact of the sound,
and in craning her neck toward it
the fact that she is not alone.
It is best to leave her there,
to step away from the pane
recalling, to return to Boyle,
that in vessels not hermetically
sealed it may be pretended
that the coldness of the internal air
is merely communicated by some
unheeded but immediate
intercourse with the external.

Experiments touching cold (2)

We often use the word freeze
in the transitive sense
to signify the operation
upon other bodies,
is what I was thinking,
or, rather, abruptly recollecting
from my reading, as it had started
to hail, so I missed the last thing
she said, and to cover that lapse
I slid open the glass door
of the deck to hear the patter
against the boards, the softer
ticking against the trees,
the worrisome tinnier clatter
on the roofs of cars, ours,
having left them on the drive,
and because we had been talking
for what must have been two hours
when the hail started to fall,
covering and recovering ground,
like a word repeated over and over
the sense of things was becoming lost
leaving only a general memory that
there was a sense behind it, a terrain
we had long mapped in our heads,
each of us starting with the position
that the other had inflicted some
measure of damage, though
perhaps less certain now,
as it had grown quite late,
of course, the conversation
growing more strident,
as the ice fell faster,

pummelling the cars,
reaching a sort of intensity
that had us now in a surprising communion
before the window, knowing
it would be clearer in the morning
when in a more sympathetic light,
perhaps after some sleep,
we would be better
positioned to stand back to assess
what might at some cost be repaired,
what we might live with.

Experiments touching bodies capable of
freezing others

It is not of great difficulty to find those
bodies that harbour this quality,
among which there are scarce any
that are not at some time susceptible,
though you have reminded me
bodies cold enough to freeze others
do not of course always have
such an appearance, particularly
at first, when one is on one's best behaviour.
It is a matter of experience
the extent to which such a quality
can develop in a body
subtly predisposed then exposed
to the right conditions, such that
such a quality might be enhanced,
drawn out, as ice by salt,
or perhaps more figuratively
the rubbing of salt in one's wounds,
as it is now clear one did not mean to do.
There may in fact be disparities
between degrees of coldness,
and in many bodies that appear at first
disposed to cold, the films of ice
are very thin, indeed, and apt
quickly to disappear given
a sufficient period and degree
of warmth. Which is to say,
in prosecution of this conjecture,
it is perhaps not unworthy
of an additional trial
of the application of some heat
should you be so disposed

to attend in full to this message
and call me back.

Experiments touching bodies indisposed to be frozen

They found liquor whose subtle parts
being by distillation brought over
and united into very spirituous liquors,
totally, or at least in great measure,
freed them temporarily from what would dispose
bodies to congeal. Such a liquor
could not itself be brought to congelation
even after two weeks in the freezer
in his flat, that bottle of Jägermeister
all that remains of what should
be a memory of an evening but is
instead, due to those subtle efforts
of such liquor, a largely blank space,
one mainly marked by the bottle's cold
but unfrozen presence, which in turn
marks her absence. Which is perhaps
why it might occur to him tonight
to open the bottle and, finding it half-full
or half-empty, depending upon one's
point of view, to drain a reasonable volume
into a glass, then drain the glass
while gazing through the front windows
to the paved walk which, having iced
during the most recent storm,
would prove as slippery and uncertain
as the reasons for the existence now
of the very absence—hers—which
acts as a kind of vacuum into which
is pulled a series of thoughts, then
a curious realisation that the glass
has been refilled, even as the bottle
left on the table sweats itself
toward room temperature. Such an image

is sufficient in fact to trigger a glimpse—
as a headlight might offer a sudden
vision of a fence or tree through
the thick erasure of the snow,
as he imagines hers must have done
when against all good sense
she left mid-storm in the middle
of the night—
of that evening: a single moment
when two people grew so warm
in their various endeavours
that they opened this very set of windows
to the sound of the hissing of snow
landing on snow they hadn't realised
had piled so high, hissing in alternation
with their rough breaths, which curled
through the cold air they had invited in,
before merging with that air to leave
not a trace even as small but clear
as the trail of the single drop
of condensation rolling down the curve
of the—when did this happen—
now empty bottle.

Experiment touching the spring and weight of the air

Imagine the air around a Body,
a particular Body,
one just entered into the room.
It is a room to which perhaps you
yourself nearly did not come
that evening, but were persuaded,
the air consisting of long, slender,
flexible agitations, whirled around
as though by the rapid motion
of Decartes' *Globuli Coelestes*,
that subtle first Element
which might drive or force out
of one's vortex all such
other agitated bodies but this one.
Now the swifter this Body
whirled around, say, to music
which filled, perhaps composed, such air,
upon, say, a floor whose furniture
had been moved to the sides,
piled with plates and other detritus,
the more the Body's—let's call them
flexible—parts urged themselves
towards you. There are those
who suppose an attractive virtue
of such rarefied air and those who
deny it to have any power at all
of attraction. But let us proceed
to the following supposition:
how rare such a Body is.
You needed only rise from the chair
to let the air carry you
to the realisation it would be impossible
that any *thing* in the world should be

divisible, that bodies would rather be
stretched beyond their own dimension
ad infinitum, as you, no longer
in the chair, felt surely to be the case,
yet now, much later, you wonder
how you can feel this way for years
then part from one another.

Drink to me only with thine eyes

is one way to begin a wedding poem
which would traditionally also use words
like *rosy lips* and maybe *wine of love*,
would of near necessity
place said wine in a glass or perhaps *goblet*
to lift toward two people such as yourselves
that one is expected to describe with a phrase
like *happy couple*—

though not this poem,
which prefers to consider less the wedding day
than the marriage, which is not one day
but a succession of days, hence in this poem
such phrases as, 'hast thou paid the electric bill',
or 'thou canst put thine own plate in the dishwasher',
or 'forsooth, how dost one of thy talent and intelligence
find it so vexing to replace a toilet paper roll?'

Of course a particularly
good wedding poem will be grounded
not just by such phrases but by an object
used for its metaphoric resonances,
an object which, if I'm to be honest,
I am still seeking in this poem,

so will stall by following in the perhaps
surprising wedding poem tradition
of mentioning death—
you must mention death
not only because it is a reminder
that you two must live together within each moment (etc.),
but because to end a line with death

means one can end the next,
as I will not, with 'upon twin souls' breath',
and you know what that means, 'souls' breath'—
I hope you both know, as I don't.
Seriously, I've no idea. Poetry is like that,
so many mysteries, as with love and marriage.
Though there is much about these, too,
that I do not know, I do know that even rarer
in a wedding poem than the word 'toilet'
to which I will not refer again except
by its absence, is a focus,
as in this poem, on the wedding registry,
as it is traditionally seen as more appropriate
to wish the couple *happiness* or *joy* or *everlasting love*,
as these are less readily found
than a waffle maker, iridescent napkin rings,
Cuisinart CFO-3SS Electric Fondue kit
or eight-piece knife set including paring, chef,
bread, carving, utility and santoku knife—

the santoku whose name you might not be aware
in Japanese means 'three virtues'.
And wouldn't we, if we could, all register
for three virtues going into a marriage?
So it turns out the santoku knife acts
as the metaphorical ground
for this wedding poem
because were I to register again
I would request any number of useful virtues,
first among them patience, forbearance, and generosity,
which is all I am saying:

the only things you really need in a marriage
are santoku, though alas we as guests

are not able to procure, to wrap or to send in lieu
such metaphorical santoku,
so these must be your gifts
to one another, when 'thine eyes'
won't quite hack it, a real drink is in order,
but the wine of love is low,
lips pressed in frustration
at dishes in the sink,
cardboard roll with its useless
last scrap of paper,
overdue notice from the electric company.

In such moments, and the many others
that make up the days of a marriage,
it is the santoku which will be your best gift
to one another, and which I recommend to you,
the—of course—happy couple,
to whom I lift my goblet,
though of course as a practical matter
I really can't help but also wish for you both
a good set of ramekins,
and, at least metaphorically,
a gravy boat.

BRASS BAND TO FOLLOW

1974

Atomic rock balls are mud formed around stone,
left to dry in the sun. They're everywhere,
we're close to the ground.
Jack has left his porch, threatened to find them
and show me what for. The air is spring entering summer,
dogwoods and cherry blossoms shedding
summer's first skin, my father already in his bed
of azaleas, laying the bodies of the bulbs, all season telling me
to fight back. Summer is years long before it begins.
I'm seven, my mother lets me wander alone along
the block though holds my hand across the street.
Jack will become my friend, then a man, then will set me aside.
He's my enemy now, though, he's just told me.
An hour from now, or a day, a week,
I will take him down in my back yard,
and my father will pull me from him
in fear of the damage I might do
and guilt over not permitting me, finally, to do it.
It won't be my last fight, though the last I will win.
I won't say I wasn't afraid that he would return,
each time I am afraid,
but the world is a wide web of green,
and I call into it, send my voice
ahead, to the future, it's never yet failed me,
and wait for my mother in the moments after
the wind has dropped, the neighbours like stones,
the paint of my parents' roof visible through the trees
on the next block, not a car passing on the blacktop,
the melting tar an ocean between us.
Forgive me, Jack, for growing up
and old and out of my body,
for the fist my father held,
a flower come loose in his hand.

Infinities

are not what they seem
or at least are not all alike,
as my precocious eight-year-old son
has recently discovered:
that one infinity
of sand granules or moments,
counterintuitive as it might seem,
really can be larger than another,
as though never ending
can be exceeded by another
never ending.
This is what we discuss
as we sit in Auckland traffic,
he in the back seat,
me gripping the wheel,
inching forward through yet
another set of traffic lights
and roundabouts,
behind the cars that line
as far as vision permits.
My point about infinity
grows more distant
even as I continue to talk and talk,
while in my head I contemplate
the shrinking number of days
he will sit in the back seat
chatting away to my reflection,
with time enough between each question
he asks and my answer to wonder
whether Gauss was right
to say infinity is not real,
just a way of speaking,

as I tried to explain to a teacher
who had taken off points,
when I was just a bit older
than my son is now,
for my response to the statement
'the grains of sand on the earth are infinite'
because it seemed to me evident that
were it possible to count them at the moment
my pencil circled the word 'false'
we would have a precise number
of grains, however small each might be
and however large their number.
I was not able to articulate
to the teacher that such a large
number only feels infinite,
like the many conversations
with my son that seem to conclude
with an infinite set of the word 'no',
or the minutes until we reach his school
this morning, or the time we have left
together, within his childhood,
though I am unable to articulate
in terms even he, smart as he is,
will understand, that at some point
you find one is not granted
an infinity of minutes, that plenitude
must be found within each of them,
something I have never been able
to grasp—viscerally, I mean—
my eyes on the destination
just beyond the last visible point
that recedes seemingly without end,
so am hardly the teacher he needs,
though at any rate some things one

simply must discover for one's self.
So the conversation, though not our car,
rolls on, about number sets
and poor Georg Cantor,
who went insane contemplating
all he could not understand
about what will never end,
and what, despite appearances,
most certainly will, something
a better father wouldn't have
mentioned, a father more capable
of exercising discretion, who does not feel
the need to fill every silence with sound
as the scenery passes, the North Shore bays,
with their beaches of not-quite endless
grains of sand, albeit slowly enough
to enjoy if one had the inclination,
however momentary, like his attention,
which will shift to something else
entirely when despite all appearances
this concludes, as it does right now,
we've arrived, he's stepping away,
but look at how I go on.

Editing

This film has been modified
from the original
to fit the screen,

to fill the screen
whose border holds the world
portrayed on the screen

in the generosity of its
cupped, greedy hands
like epistemological limits

dictating what to think about
or not or what's not worth
thinking about, the truth

being that it is much like the original,
with only a few modifications,
though, since you press me,

since you seem, and I say this,
as you used to say, *descriptively,*
without intention to judge,

obsessed with minor modifications,
much has, it turns out, changed.
Your good shoes are gathering

dust. Your husband has rearranged
the photographs framing
the mantle. Below your window,

if you would take a look,
if from some strange world
beyond the borders of this one

you can still look, or care to,
day has stamped night
into the shape of a small boy's

shadow. You'd hate it,
this film with its minor
dramas, not the expansive

cast of thousands seen
from above leaving their
homes, their orchards

and crops for parts unknown,
would be dismayed to learn
the portico you'd carefully

constructed for the thin
bookends of summer work
weeks is packed with possessions

you would hardly recognise,
no longer in their long-standing
positions in fixed orbit

around the gravity you
engendered even while making
light. What, one wonders,

would you make of the new
planet discovered leaning
behind Pluto like a waiter

on a smoke break, the new
thinking on the evolution
of the universe? The external

pressure of our atmosphere
has modified the shape
of your face, but it's nothing

serious and will become less so
in the years after your disappearance.
Welcome to the years

after your disappearance.
We've missed you here.
We've been looking

at photographs, still
vibrant with what has changed:
our feelings for you, for example,

since the world goes on behind
your back and better than ever,
and having dug the trench

of your absence, you're no longer
as we imagined, those of us
here in the modified

world so like the original,
just different enough
to accommodate

a perspective just
a bit smaller without
you here to mock

our mouths still
flapping like leaves,
some forgotten field.

Laundry

It is like all hazy transitions—dusk, autumn,
decline—this move from back to basket,
the renaming of the best blouse, linen shirt,
long underwear, the burden of this new
name borne by those things which have
outlived, for now, their usefulness
and must be reborn,
baptised back into the fold.

A misstep into a mud puddle,
a ruptured vein of ink,
the rolling path of a nosebleed,
the irrefutable streak of Sunday's sexual desire.

Only once each pair of jeans is crisply folded,
every pair of panties packed in a drawer,
each cotton shirt lifted to hanger,
do they recover the potential inherent
in that word—clothing—
as in that instant, after we wake,
when sunlight bathes the room, and filth
is a foreign country, another language.

Eternity

Or maybe there is no final film
flashing in your last minute,
just the underside of a pine
lid to stare into every minute
thereafter, its grain a screen
on which to view your life,
whatever it has been,
at any speed you like,
to forward at first through the dull,
slow spaces, but to eventually
understand these frames pull
the others together, to replay
each of them second by cold
second: the rough hem
of a dress, the bare overhead
light in a strange washroom,
a winter landscape inside an empty
cereal box, a ladder's
rusting rung, the unending
grey of an office divider.

Organ Donation

A woman with a dead man's heart swore she'd
picked up a taste for fried onions and black beer,

found herself nights in a pub passed a hundred times
never imagining the inside, now ordering pints,

letting her nose linger over greasy waxed paper,
her forefinger rub the corners. It must have been

in his blood—his taste, his yearning for the world.
A walk through snow, the scent of Sunday,

the creak of Italian leather—are these the desires we pass
to one another summer nights, the air calling cool

through the sill, drapes flapping like flags? I took
a late swim at the beach with a girl once. We were naked

and not concealed by night as I imagined when
I made the suggestion I'd imagined she would refuse.

I'm offering you that bay, the way the crescent moon
broke the surface of the sky, the ginger on her tongue

in the warm lapping night, and the way I delay
a glass below my lips as I speak, a voice

that wakes you to find it is merely April
through the window, a dream faded before you've shut it.

Snapshot

Light touches the vase
then your eyes as you sit
on the couch, my fingers
stretched to cover the distance
of an instant from which
we spin on an axis
whose orbit decays even
the way we look at ourselves,
memory slipping,
the flower whose name
when you are asked by a child
has spilled with its seed,
time a scythe through a field
around a bucket
that lies on its side,
tomatoes tumbling out
like days at the end
of the summer my father
painted that scene from a photograph,
an image he fears failed
to capture the curve of the fruit
or noon bounding off the side
of the pail or the peal
of the lunch bell
that sent the gatherer
hopping the frame like a fence
that captures nothing,
the way a mirror bounces
back an image which travels
a distance twice, and time,
always faster than light,
makes us that much

older than we look,
the closest we come.

On Saturday

I pause before my window
to catch an angle

of afternoon light
lost during the week,

slow enough
to see the mind work,

how easily
distracted by a child

and old man on a walk,
the way they stop

to watch a last sunlit
leaf float from a branch.

My leaves in childhood
slipped on the air,

hovered above my hand
as slim as chance,

though later I watched
from my room as they

cut down the oak, entranced
at how its absence

emptied a space for the sun
to stretch and awaken

with its touch the empty
patch that would

the next and every season
be the grass I would cut,

until the last pull of mower
across the lawn

severed summer from
what was to come:

a shaving of days,
then the snow

sweeping in from the side,
as it sweeps in

tonight, piling on familiar
paths, turning trees to memories

more imagined than recalled.
Now I can barely see

the flakes against the streetlights
that fade to my reflection,

a man fading in with night,
the outlines of his life

burning behind him,
the laundry done.

Smoke

It rises above the house, beyond weatherboards that will not hold paint
against the sun's seasonal slap, against which in turn is posed
all manner of protection upon the girl and boy who run in the yard.
Autumn, the wood is stacked, they run around and around all the world
they have known: flax, lemonwood shading out the saplings
of the self-seeded oak, the tree whose cherries, like the greengage plums,
like the apricots in the tallest branches, feed the strange birds that land
among these very lines, which will not contain what won't be captured:
the smoke of a woodburner whose hunger must be fed
and fed, season after lean season, a nervous eye cast over
diminishing arcs of wood. The wish to release and keep, security
and diminishment inextricable. It rises over the yard where the girl
chases the boy until they round the house older than they have
a right by memory to be. See the tūī flit through their lives,
the fantail in the garden, the sheep in the paddock, and here again
from around the house the girl and boy come running in tears,
come running in laughter, must be told to slow down, take it easy,
come to bed, get up, draw a bath, be nice. It rises higher
as though buoyed by the collective breaths of those mowing many lawns
in patterns so diffuse and contradictory as to belie all sense of what
from the ground are called paths. Become its rise until the yard
is a stamp, the shape of a map of the past, where a man forever sits
wondering how he got to a place he will never understand but to which
he has given all he had to give: a smoke that is renewed
even as it gives part of itself to the vagaries of the winds with all their
many monikers, the currents that carry what must be carried,
a smoke whose ungraspable tendrils, the definition of haze,
nevertheless hover or float in what from a distance seems
for a tantalising moment to hold the solidity of shape,
before dispersing itself over the oral history of the firehouse,
the archeological layers of the schoolyard, past the orbs piled
in their glowing prime in the bins of the market garden,

then, if only as a scent beyond sensing, across to parts
unknown. See the girl and boy, the backs of their heads,
their faces hidden in the shadow cast by a future only they will know,
a future they must follow one another into, what you want, what you don't,
past the gate that will not contain what must move beyond
our will to hold it still, and close.

The value of a statistical life

is what I am reading about in the news
on this lazy Sunday morning,
with the lawn in need of a mow,
a chance of rain that, for now, holds off,
the scent of French toast lingering,
like us, in the rooms. Technically speaking,
it is the marginal rate of substitution
between wealth and mortality risk,
a calculation of the chances of death
and how much we're willing
to give up to prevent it.
Somewhere in the garage,
helmets we purchased to protect the heads
of our children hang on handlebars,
but right now my son worries a Rubik's cube,
my daughter is playing a sonatina,
holding back a bit on her dynamics
with a caution I worry she has learned from me.
The value of a statistical life, calculated
from a reasonable distance, assumes
that as individuals maximise
their expected utility in various ways,
under alternative states of the world,
we can calculate the slope of an indifference curve.
Are such curves proportional to the volume
of news we receive on states of the world?
I read it will take two years to identify thousands
of immigrant children separated from parents.
After a statistical analysis of 47,000 children
they will review only cases with the highest probability.
I have been too cautious, I think, with my own children.
What do they know, really, about the impossible

choices a parent thousands of miles from here
never anticipated on a Sunday morning like this
yet now must make about cutting through
a fence or sending a child on alone,
about the many difficult borders my daughter's
own great-grandparents crossed so we could
sit here so comfortably, all of us, a series
of chance factors whose points graph a curve
far beyond any value I can gauge?
The statistical values of Jewish and Muslim
lives, white lives and black, the old and young.
What price the curve of indifference?
Two children detained at the border
die from a flu that a simple jab
they were denied would have prevented.
A man is arrested for providing two
statistical lives food and water in the desert.
Will it get better or worse.
Is there a marginal utility to love.
How much time do we have to maximise it,
a Sunday morning climbing note by note
into an afternoon I wish to hold off
by holding on, just as I wish to hold off the moment,
not too far now, when my daughter pushes back
the piano bench one final time to cross
the porous border into the perilous country
of her own full life, and hold off, too,
even today's simple pleasure
of moving a mower through my own lawn,
as I look again through the window,
clouds hovering over the safety of this yard,
for any sign of a change in the weather,
any gathering darkness, for some distance
from which one might comfortably
calculate the unimaginable odds.

Brass band to follow

it says on the banner hung
on the cart towed before us
by the green John Deere
whose driver waves to us
like any hero. The girls swoop
by dressed as elves, tossing
hard candies to the kids
as the world's floats pass.
My son, who last year sat
on my shoulders for this spectacle,
sweats in a straw costume
with a dozen others in the bed of a ute
way down the road to where it bends.
This was what he had been looking
forward to, finally, his earned place
in the village Christmas parade,
where every industrial machine,
emergency vehicle, mechanic's van,
old-time automobile bearing
the local real estate firm's banner,
is transformed by paper mâché
and an overheated, slumped Santa
with his yellowing beard into something
meant to be larger than itself,
the crowd elbow-to-elbow on Cambridge
Avenue as the season variously salutes,
saunters, sashays past, settles
itself in, the start of a long summer,
or so the Met Service has suggested,
though they said the same thing last year.
Nearly noon, rides and booths set up
at the community centre, the scent

of sausages, the young girls on horses
now, followed by the Girl Guides,
in their pink singlets, war veterans,
the sun burnishing the fire engine
as it rolls past. Then the silvered metal
of the truck at last in which my son sits,
looking suddenly uncertain, like someone
staring down at a meal he is unsure
he has ordered in a country whose
language he does not yet speak,
while my wife and I wave and wave
and wait, like him, for all that has been
forecast to be fulfilled, for what
has been written to come, to pass.

Notes

Much of the language in the 'Micrographia' series is taken from *Micrographia: or Some Physiological Descriptions of Minute Bodies Made by Magnifying Glasses. With Observations and Inquiries Thereupon* (1665) by the scientist Robert Hooke (1635–1703), who coined the term 'cell'. It was the first work to relate observations of nature and other objects through the microscope.

Much of the language in the 'Experiments Touching Cold' series comes from *New experiments and observations touching cold, or, An experimental history of cold begun to which are added an examen of antiperistasis and an examen of Mr. Hobs's doctrine about cold* (1665) by the scientist Robert Boyle (1627–1691). Boyle was one of the pioneers of modern chemistry (known for 'Boyle's Law'), seeking the precision of measurement and scientific experiment. Much of the language in the last poem in the series comes from *A defence of the doctrine touching the spring and weight of the air propos'd by Mr. R. Boyle in his new physico-mechanical experiments, against the objections of Franciscus Linus; wherewith the objector's funicular hypothesis is also examin'd, by the author of those experiments* (1662).

The title 'Drink to me only with thine eyes' is the first line from 'Song to Celia' by Ben Jonson (1572–1637). The line 'wine of love' is from the poem 'The Wine of Love' by James Thomson (1834–1882).

'Gross Anatomy' is for Zev Waldman. 'Relativities' is for Tim Upperton.

'Drink to me only with thine eyes' is for Matt and Stacee.

Acknowledgements

Thanks are due to the editors of the following publications in which some of these poems first appeared, sometimes in different form: *Ika, Geometry, Landfall, Poetry New Zealand, takahē*. 'Transporting' appeared in *2001: A Science Fiction Poetry Anthology* (Anamnesis Press, 2001). 'Tranquil' was a finalist in the 2017 Montreal Poetry Prize and appeared in the *Montreal Poetry Prize Global Poetry Anthology* (Véhicule Press, 2017). 'Smoke' was published in the 2015 Montreal Poetry Prize Longlist.

I am grateful to Massey University for teaching release to work on some of these poems. My gratitude, too, to Lynley Edmeades for her suggestions and her eagle eye. My greatest thanks to my parents for their ongoing support, to my children for their wonder, and to Nancy Golubiewski for believing.